MW00887824

THANK YOU FOR YOUR PURCHASE

SIGNUP
FOR A FREE
Gift

mgpublish.com/free-download/

We hope you enjoy this book.

All feedback is greatly appreciated as it lets
us know how we are doing!

For any inquiries please feel free to email us at
contact@mgpublish.com

THIS BOOK BELONGS TO:

CONTACT INFORMATION

NAME:
_____

ADDRESS:
_____
_____
_____

PHONE:
_____

START / END DATES

/   /   TO   /   /
_____   _____

BUSINESS DETAILS

BUSINESS NAME:	
ADDRESS:	
EMAIL ADDRESS:	**PHONE NUMBER:**
FAX NUMBER:	**WEBSITE:**

LOGBOOK DETAILS

CONTINUED FROM LOGBOOK:	
CONTINUED TO LOGBOOK:	
DATE LOG STARTED:	**DATE LOG ENDED:**

NOTES

LIVESTOCK RECORD

DATE:		START DATE:			END OF YEAR:			
NO	TYPE OF LIVESTOCK	QTY	AVG WEIGHT	VALUE	QTY	AVG WEIGHT	VALUE	BALANCE

BUSINESS DETAILS

BUSINESS NAME:	
ADDRESS:	
EMAIL ADDRESS:	PHONE NUMBER:
FAX NUMBER:	WEBSITE:

LOGBOOK DETAILS

CONTINUED FROM LOGBOOK:	
CONTINUED TO LOGBOOK:	
DATE LOG STARTED:	DATE LOG ENDED:

NOTES

LIVESTOCK RECORD

DATE:		START DATE:			END OF YEAR:			
NO	TYPE OF LIVESTOCK	QTY	AVG WEIGHT	VALUE	QTY	AVG WEIGHT	VALUE	BALANCE

LIVESTOCK RECORD

DATE:		START DATE:			END OF YEAR:			
NO	TYPE OF LIVESTOCK	QTY	AVG WEIGHT	VALUE	QTY	AVG WEIGHT	VALUE	BALANCE

FARM EXPENSES

MONTH: _____

DATE	EXPENSES	COST	REMARKS

FARM EXPENSES

DATE	EXPENSES	COST	REMARKS

TOTAL:

FARM INCOME

MONTH: _____

DATE	SOURCE	DESCRIPTION	METHOD OF PAYMENT	AMOUNT

FARM INCOME

DATE	SOURCE	DESCRIPTION	METHOD OF PAYMENT	AMOUNT
			TOTAL:	

EQUIPMENT MAINTENANCE & REPAIR

MONTH: _____

DATE	EQUIPMENT	INSPECTION | MAINTENANCE REPAIR | SERVICES REQUIRED	SERVICE|REPAIR DATE	INITIALS	REMARKS

NOTES

LIVESTOCK RECORD

DATE:		START DATE:			END OF YEAR:			
NO	**TYPE OF LIVESTOCK**	**QTY**	**AVG WEIGHT**	**VALUE**	**QTY**	**AVG WEIGHT**	**VALUE**	**BALANCE**

LIVESTOCK RECORD

DATE:		START DATE:			END OF YEAR:			
NO	TYPE OF LIVESTOCK	QTY	AVG WEIGHT	VALUE	QTY	AVG WEIGHT	VALUE	BALANCE

FARM EXPENSES

MONTH: _____

DATE	EXPENSES	COST	REMARKS

FARM EXPENSES

DATE	EXPENSES	COST	REMARKS

TOTAL:

FARM INCOME

MONTH: _____

DATE	SOURCE	DESCRIPTION	METHOD OF PAYMENT	AMOUNT

FARM INCOME

DATE	SOURCE	DESCRIPTION	METHOD OF PAYMENT	AMOUNT
			TOTAL:	

EQUIPMENT MAINTENANCE & REPAIR

MONTH: _____

DATE	EQUIPMENT	INSPECTION | MAINTENANCE REPAIR | SERVICES REQUIRED	SERVICE | REPAIR DATE	INITIALS	REMARKS

NOTES

LIVESTOCK RECORD

		START DATE:			END OF YEAR:			
DATE:								
NO	TYPE OF LIVESTOCK	QTY	AVG WEIGHT	VALUE	QTY	AVG WEIGHT	VALUE	BALANCE

LIVESTOCK RECORD

DATE:		START DATE:			END OF YEAR:			
NO	**TYPE OF LIVESTOCK**	**QTY**	**AVG WEIGHT**	**VALUE**	**QTY**	**AVG WEIGHT**	**VALUE**	**BALANCE**

FARM EXPENSES

MONTH: _____

DATE	EXPENSES	COST	REMARKS

FARM EXPENSES

DATE	EXPENSES	COST	REMARKS

TOTAL:

FARM INCOME

MONTH: _____

DATE	SOURCE	DESCRIPTION	METHOD OF PAYMENT	AMOUNT

FARM INCOME

DATE	SOURCE	DESCRIPTION	METHOD OF PAYMENT	AMOUNT
			TOTAL:	

EQUIPMENT MAINTENANCE & REPAIR

MONTH: _____

DATE	EQUIPMENT	INSPECTION | MAINTENANCE REPAIR | SERVICES REQUIRED	SERVICE | REPAIR DATE	INITIALS	REMARKS

NOTES

LIVESTOCK RECORD

DATE: | **START DATE:** | **END OF YEAR:**

NO	TYPE OF LIVESTOCK	QTY	AVG WEIGHT	VALUE	QTY	AVG WEIGHT	VALUE	BALANCE

LIVESTOCK RECORD

DATE:		START DATE:			END OF YEAR:			
NO	TYPE OF LIVESTOCK	QTY	AVG WEIGHT	VALUE	QTY	AVG WEIGHT	VALUE	BALANCE

FARM EXPENSES

MONTH: _____

DATE	EXPENSES	COST	REMARKS

FARM EXPENSES

DATE	EXPENSES	COST	REMARKS

TOTAL:

FARM INCOME

MONTH: _____

DATE	SOURCE	DESCRIPTION	METHOD OF PAYMENT	AMOUNT

FARM INCOME

DATE	SOURCE	DESCRIPTION	METHOD OF PAYMENT	AMOUNT
			TOTAL:	

EQUIPMENT MAINTENANCE & REPAIR

MONTH: _____

DATE	EQUIPMENT	INSPECTION | MAINTENANCE REPAIR | SERVICES REQUIRED	SERVICE | REPAIR DATE	INITIALS	REMARKS

NOTES

LIVESTOCK RECORD

DATE:		START DATE:			END OF YEAR:			
NO	TYPE OF LIVESTOCK	QTY	AVG WEIGHT	VALUE	QTY	AVG WEIGHT	VALUE	BALANCE

LIVESTOCK RECORD

DATE:		START DATE:			END OF YEAR:			
NO	TYPE OF LIVESTOCK	QTY	AVG WEIGHT	VALUE	QTY	AVG WEIGHT	VALUE	BALANCE

FARM EXPENSES

MONTH: _____

DATE	EXPENSES	COST	REMARKS

FARM EXPENSES

DATE	EXPENSES	COST	REMARKS
	TOTAL:		

FARM INCOME

MONTH: _____

DATE	SOURCE	DESCRIPTION	METHOD OF PAYMENT	AMOUNT

FARM INCOME

DATE	SOURCE	DESCRIPTION	METHOD OF PAYMENT	AMOUNT
			TOTAL:	

EQUIPMENT MAINTENANCE & REPAIR

MONTH: _____

DATE	EQUIPMENT	INSPECTION | MAINTENANCE REPAIR | SERVICES REQUIRED	SERVICE | REPAIR DATE	INITIALS	REMARKS

NOTES

LIVESTOCK RECORD

DATE:		START DATE:			END OF YEAR:			
NO	TYPE OF LIVESTOCK	QTY	AVG WEIGHT	VALUE	QTY	AVG WEIGHT	VALUE	BALANCE

LIVESTOCK RECORD

DATE:		START DATE:			END OF YEAR:			
NO	TYPE OF LIVESTOCK	QTY	AVG WEIGHT	VALUE	QTY	AVG WEIGHT	VALUE	BALANCE

FARM EXPENSES

MONTH: _____

DATE	EXPENSES	COST	REMARKS

FARM EXPENSES

DATE	EXPENSES	COST	REMARKS

TOTAL:

FARM INCOME

MONTH: _____

DATE	SOURCE	DESCRIPTION	METHOD OF PAYMENT	AMOUNT

FARM INCOME

DATE	SOURCE	DESCRIPTION	METHOD OF PAYMENT	AMOUNT
			TOTAL:	

EQUIPMENT MAINTENANCE & REPAIR

MONTH: _____

DATE	EQUIPMENT	INSPECTION | MAINTENANCE REPAIR | SERVICES REQUIRED	SERVICE | REPAIR DATE	INITIALS	REMARKS

NOTES

LIVESTOCK RECORD

DATE:		START DATE:			END OF YEAR:			
NO	TYPE OF LIVESTOCK	QTY	AVG WEIGHT	VALUE	QTY	AVG WEIGHT	VALUE	BALANCE

LIVESTOCK RECORD

DATE:		START DATE:			END OF YEAR:			
NO	TYPE OF LIVESTOCK	QTY	AVG WEIGHT	VALUE	QTY	AVG WEIGHT	VALUE	BALANCE

FARM EXPENSES

MONTH: _____

DATE	EXPENSES	COST	REMARKS

FARM EXPENSES

DATE	EXPENSES	COST	REMARKS
	TOTAL:		

FARM INCOME

MONTH: _____

DATE	SOURCE	DESCRIPTION	METHOD OF PAYMENT	AMOUNT

FARM INCOME

DATE	SOURCE	DESCRIPTION	METHOD OF PAYMENT	AMOUNT
			TOTAL:	

EQUIPMENT MAINTENANCE & REPAIR

MONTH: _____

DATE	EQUIPMENT	INSPECTION | MAINTENANCE REPAIR | SERVICES REQUIRED	SERVICE | REPAIR DATE	INITIALS	REMARKS

NOTES

LIVESTOCK RECORD

DATE:		START DATE:			END OF YEAR:			
NO	TYPE OF LIVESTOCK	QTY	AVG WEIGHT	VALUE	QTY	AVG WEIGHT	VALUE	BALANCE

LIVESTOCK RECORD

DATE:		START DATE:			END OF YEAR:			
NO	TYPE OF LIVESTOCK	QTY	AVG WEIGHT	VALUE	QTY	AVG WEIGHT	VALUE	BALANCE

FARM EXPENSES

MONTH: _____

DATE	EXPENSES	COST	REMARKS

FARM EXPENSES

DATE	EXPENSES	COST	REMARKS
	TOTAL:		

FARM INCOME

MONTH: _____

DATE	SOURCE	DESCRIPTION	METHOD OF PAYMENT	AMOUNT

FARM INCOME

DATE	SOURCE	DESCRIPTION	METHOD OF PAYMENT	AMOUNT
			TOTAL:	

EQUIPMENT MAINTENANCE & REPAIR

MONTH: _____

DATE	EQUIPMENT	INSPECTION | MAINTENANCE REPAIR | SERVICES REQUIRED	SERVICE | REPAIR DATE	INITIALS	REMARKS

NOTES

LIVESTOCK RECORD

DATE:		START DATE:			END OF YEAR:			
NO	TYPE OF LIVESTOCK	QTY	AVG WEIGHT	VALUE	QTY	AVG WEIGHT	VALUE	BALANCE

LIVESTOCK RECORD

DATE:		START DATE:			END OF YEAR:			
NO	TYPE OF LIVESTOCK	QTY	AVG WEIGHT	VALUE	QTY	AVG WEIGHT	VALUE	BALANCE

FARM EXPENSES

MONTH: _____

DATE	EXPENSES	COST	REMARKS

FARM EXPENSES

DATE	EXPENSES	COST	REMARKS

TOTAL:

FARM INCOME

MONTH: _____

DATE	SOURCE	DESCRIPTION	METHOD OF PAYMENT	AMOUNT

FARM INCOME

DATE	SOURCE	DESCRIPTION	METHOD OF PAYMENT	AMOUNT
			TOTAL:	

EQUIPMENT MAINTENANCE & REPAIR

MONTH: _____

DATE	EQUIPMENT	INSPECTION | MAINTENANCE REPAIR | SERVICES REQUIRED	SERVICE | REPAIR DATE	INITIALS	REMARKS

NOTES

LIVESTOCK RECORD

		START DATE:			END OF YEAR:			
DATE:								
NO	TYPE OF LIVESTOCK	QTY	AVG WEIGHT	VALUE	QTY	AVG WEIGHT	VALUE	BALANCE

LIVESTOCK RECORD

DATE:		START DATE:			END OF YEAR:			
NO	TYPE OF LIVESTOCK	QTY	AVG WEIGHT	VALUE	QTY	AVG WEIGHT	VALUE	BALANCE

FARM EXPENSES

MONTH: _____

DATE	EXPENSES	COST	REMARKS

FARM EXPENSES

DATE	EXPENSES	COST	REMARKS
	TOTAL:		

FARM INCOME

MONTH: _____

DATE	SOURCE	DESCRIPTION	METHOD OF PAYMENT	AMOUNT

FARM INCOME

DATE	SOURCE	DESCRIPTION	METHOD OF PAYMENT	AMOUNT
			TOTAL:	

EQUIPMENT MAINTENANCE & REPAIR

MONTH: _____

DATE	EQUIPMENT	INSPECTION | MAINTENANCE REPAIR | SERVICES REQUIRED	SERVICE | REPAIR DATE	INITIALS	REMARKS

NOTES

LIVESTOCK RECORD

DATE:		START DATE:			END OF YEAR:			
NO	TYPE OF LIVESTOCK	QTY	AVG WEIGHT	VALUE	QTY	AVG WEIGHT	VALUE	BALANCE

LIVESTOCK RECORD

DATE:		START DATE:			END OF YEAR:			
NO	TYPE OF LIVESTOCK	QTY	AVG WEIGHT	VALUE	QTY	AVG WEIGHT	VALUE	BALANCE

FARM EXPENSES

MONTH: _____

DATE	EXPENSES	COST	REMARKS

FARM EXPENSES

DATE	EXPENSES	COST	REMARKS

TOTAL:

FARM INCOME

MONTH: _____

DATE	SOURCE	DESCRIPTION	METHOD OF PAYMENT	AMOUNT

FARM INCOME

DATE	SOURCE	DESCRIPTION	METHOD OF PAYMENT	AMOUNT
			TOTAL:	

EQUIPMENT MAINTENANCE & REPAIR

MONTH: _____

DATE	EQUIPMENT	INSPECTION | MAINTENANCE REPAIR | SERVICES REQUIRED	SERVICE | REPAIR DATE	INITIALS	REMARKS

NOTES

LIVESTOCK RECORD

		DATE:	START DATE:		END OF YEAR:			
NO	TYPE OF LIVESTOCK	QTY	AVG WEIGHT	VALUE	QTY	AVG WEIGHT	VALUE	BALANCE

LIVESTOCK RECORD

DATE:		START DATE:			END OF YEAR:			
NO	TYPE OF LIVESTOCK	QTY	AVG WEIGHT	VALUE	QTY	AVG WEIGHT	VALUE	BALANCE

FARM EXPENSES

MONTH: _____

DATE	EXPENSES	COST	REMARKS

FARM EXPENSES

DATE	EXPENSES	COST	REMARKS

TOTAL:

FARM INCOME

MONTH: _____

DATE	SOURCE	DESCRIPTION	METHOD OF PAYMENT	AMOUNT

FARM INCOME

DATE	SOURCE	DESCRIPTION	METHOD OF PAYMENT	AMOUNT
			TOTAL:	

EQUIPMENT MAINTENANCE & REPAIR

MONTH: _____

DATE	EQUIPMENT	INSPECTION | MAINTENANCE REPAIR | SERVICES REQUIRED	SERVICE | REPAIR DATE	INITIALS	REMARKS

NOTES

NOTES

Made in the USA
Monee, IL
15 December 2024

73730604R00057